THE OFFICIAL
SCOTLAND
FOOTBALL
ANNUAL 2010

Written by Roddy Mackenzie
Contributions: Graeme Booth, Al Watt,
Michael Mackenzie

A Grange Publication

© 2009. Published by Grange Communications Ltd.,
Edinburgh, under licence from The Scottish Football
Association. Printed in the EU.

Photographs © SNSPix, The Scottish FA,
The Scottish Football Museum

ISBN 978-1-907104-19-0

£6.99

CONTENTS

7   Introduction

8   A Day in the Life, George Burley

10   Group Nine, A Look Back

14   Instant Recall

15   Wordsearch

16   Scotland Greats

26   Quiz

27   Wordsearch

28   The Next Batch

32   Thanks for the Memories

38   Spotlight on the Fans

43   Stateside with Ifeoma Dieke

46   Midfield Maestros

52   Living with the Auld Enemy

56   One-Cap Wonders

59   Tartan Trivia

61   Answers

INTRODUCTION

Welcome to the second official Scotland Annual and another publication packed with everything you need to know about following the national team.

There is a look back to celebrate some of the great players who have worn the dark blue with distinction and who each made a unique contribution to the rich tapestry of our team – who was the "Wee Blue Devil"? Who won 102 caps for his country? Who had the audacity to play "keepie-uppie" on the Wembley turf just months after England won the World Cup? We also look back on some of Scotland's greatest games in our trip down memory lane – some more recent than others. What do Alfie Conn, Keith Wright and Robbie Winters have in common? The answer is supplied later in this annual.

National team manager George Burley gives us an exclusive insight into his preparations for a big match. Billy Stark also takes time out to give us his thoughts about what he believes young footballers should have in their locker.
There are the usual quizzes and word searches to test your Tartan Army credentials in another packed publication which is a must for every Scotland fan.

A Day in The Life - George Burley

BEING SCOTLAND MANAGER IS THE GREATEST JOB IN THE WORLD. NOT ONLY DO I GET TO WORK WITH THE PLAYERS AS WE TRY AND TAKE OUR COUNTRY TO THE WORLD CUP AND THE OTHER BIG EVENTS LIKE THE EUROPEAN CHAMPIONSHIPS, I ALSO GET TO WATCH A LOT OF FOOTBALL! IT IS A DREAM JOB - AND ONE THAT I AM REALLY PROUD TO HAVE. I PLAYED FOR SCOTLAND AT EVERY LEVEL AND I WENT TO THE WORLD CUP IN 1982. I KNOW WHAT IT MEANS TO BE A SCOTLAND FAN AND THAT IS WHY I KNOW JUST HOW IMPORTANT IT IS TO EVERYONE THAT WE WIN OUR GAMES AND GET TO THE BIGGEST EVENTS.

A LOT OF PEOPLE WORK REALLY HARD ON AND OFF THE PITCH TO MAKE SURE THAT WE GET THE RIGHT RESULTS FOR THE FANS. AS WELL AS ALL THE TRAINING, WE HAVE TO HAVE PRESS CONFERENCES AND CHARITY EVENTS IN THE BUILD UP TO MATCHES. THIS IS REALLY IMPORTANT AS IT MEANS THAT EVERYONE IN SCOTLAND IS KEPT INFORMED WITH WHAT IS GOING ON.

SO, IF YOU WANTED TO KNOW WHAT GOES ON BEHIND THE SCENES IN THE BUILD UP TO A BIG MATCH - LOOK NO FURTHER.

GEORGE

MONDAY

The game is on Saturday - so the players will be getting together tonight at the team hotel. When they get there, they will all be looked at by the team medical staff to see how they are. If there are any players with injuries or knocks, the doctors have a look at them and see what work needs to be done. During the day, I do my first press conference of the week. It is always really busy as all the journalists try to find out who is going to be in the team. I like to keep that a secret though! If people in Scotland find out who is going to be in my team from the newspapers, you can be sure that the opposition manager will find out too!

TUESDAY

All the players are now with us and we have our first training session of the week. I love being at training as it gives you a chance to work on new ideas with the players and to start working on how we are going to win the match. The players are a great bunch of boys and they always make training good fun.

WEDNESDAY

It is press conference number two! This time we invite all the journalists to the team hotel and, as well as speaking to me or Terry, they get to speak to some of the players. I know that a lot of the boys don't feel comfortable speaking to the press a lot of the times, but they understand how important it is to let the supporters know what is going on. So they all do it - although they may need a bit of persuading..! In the afternoon it is training again - and this time we invite some of our charities along to meet the players. Everyone always loves this and we always have a good time with the supporters who come along. Scotland fans love their team - and I love spending time with them.

THURSDAY

We are now down to the serious business of the match. Training is much more intensive as I start to work on the team and our tactics for the match. With just a couple of days to go, training is closed - which means that no-one is allowed to sneak in to watch! It is not all serious stuff though. At night, the boys like to play on the Playstation and the Wii and we sometimes have quiz nights. As you would expect with the boys, it is always really competitive and everyone wants to beat everyone else. I like the quizzes - but I am no use with the video games. I leave all that to the players!

FRIDAY

More training - and press conference number three! This time, myself and the captain speak to the press. It is the last opportunity for the journalists before the game so they make sure they ask as many questions as they can. We then make sure that the boys are properly rested ahead of the big game. We make sure that they get an early night and are ready to go in the morning.

SATURDAY

It's match day and after breakfast we all go for a walk. We then have a team meeting, where we have a good talk about the match ahead. After a light lunch it is off to the stadium for the match. We always have a DVD on the bus of great Scotland moments. It always gets the players wound up and excited for the game.
Once we get to the stadium, the players warm up and I have to speak to the people who are showing the match live. We are then ready to go.

A Day in The Life - George Burley

Scotland have been locked in a fierce battle with Holland, Norway, Macedonia and Iceland in a bid to qualify for the World Cup in South Africa in 2010. Here, we look back on the trail so far…

MACEDONIA 1 SCOTLAND 0

Scotland started the qualification process for World Cup 2010 back on September 6, 2008, in Skopje, Macedonia. It was not the start they were hoping for.

Only five minutes into George Burley's first competitive match in charge, and Scotland fell behind in the scorching afternoon heat. In the first of a few decisions that upset them, Czech referee Pavel Kralovec blew for a soft free-kick on the edge of the area for a foul on Goran Maznov.

Craig Gordon did well to tip Goce Sedloski's effort from the set piece onto the post, but Ilcho Naumoski beat a static defence to the ball and fired home.

In a first half with little to excite the visiting fans, half chances came and went, but it was Macedonia who came closest to scoring again, with only a last-ditch tackle by Gary Caldwell preventing Maznov from doubling the lead. Scotland were an improved side after the break, but could not create a clear-cut opportunity, indeed we had Gordon to thank for keeping them in the game just before the hour mark, saving Veliche Shumulikoski's stinging strike.

The major talking point of the match came with 20 minutes to go: firstly'; Kenny Miller appeared to be tripped by Igor Mitreski, and then Petar Milosevski brought down James McFadden in the box. Either challenge could have been penalised on another day, but Kralovec waved away the appeals and booked McFadden for his protests.

Substitute Shaun Maloney came closest to an equaliser late on, but as his shot was turned away, with it went Scotland's chance of getting a point from the match.

MACEDONIA: Milosevski, Noveski, Petrov (Grncarov 78), Sedloski, Mitreski, Lazarevski, Georgievski, Shumulikoski, Maznov, Pandev (Tasevski 82), Naumoski (Trajanov 69). **Subs Not Used:** Pacovski, Polozani, Demiri, Ristic.

SCOTLAND: Gordon, Alexander, Naysmith, McManus, Caldwell, Hartley (Commons 65), Darren Fletcher, Brown, Miller (Boyd 80), McFadden, Robson (Maloney 76). **Subs Not Used:** McGregor, Broadfoot, Stewart, Berra.

ICELAND 1 SCOTLAND 2

After the disappointment of defeat in Macedonia, Scotland did not have to wait long to get their first points of the campaign, and George Burley's first win as Scotland manager.

By defeating Iceland 2-1 in Reykjavik the Scots kept up their 100% record against their hosts, but were made to work for their win.

The opening stages were dominated by the home side - Craig Gordon saved well from Aron Gunnarsson with Heidar Helguson and Eidur Gudjohnsen also going close early on.

It was therefore against the run of play that Scotland broke the deadlock in the 18th minute. Debutant Kirk Broadfoot met Barry Robson's corner with a perfectly timed run, and his bullet header beat 'keeper Kjartan Sturluson and a defender on the line.

Barcelona striker Gudjohnsen was posing a threat at one end, with James McFadden doing the same at the other, as the match began to open up. Just before the interval Stephen McManus cleared a Herman Hreidarsson effort off the line to maintain the visitor's slender advantage.

Once again it was while Iceland were bossing the match that Scotland broke up the other end and made it 2-0. After Kristjan Orn Sigurdsson needlessly fouled McFadden in the area, McFadden's penalty was saved by Sturluson, but the Birmingham man followed up to poke home with Robson also in attendance.

Stephen McManus gifted Iceland a lifeline by handling in the area and was sent off for the offence. Gudjohnsen dispatched the penalty with aplomb, setting up a nervous last 13 minutes, but Scotland held on.

ICELAND: Sturluson, Birkir Mar Saevarsson (Gunnarson 77), Eiriksson (Indridi Sigurdsson 46), Kristjan Orn Sigurdsson, Gunnarsson (Palmason 63), Steinsson, Hreidarsson, Gislason, Gudjohnsen, Helguson, Hallfredsson. **Subs Not Used:** Torgeirsson, Ragnar Sigurdsson, Thordarson, Thorvaldsson.

SCOTLAND: Gordon, Broadfoot, Naysmith, McManus, Caldwell, Brown, Darren Fletcher, Maloney (Alexander 78), McFadden (Hartley 80), Robson, Commons (Miller 62). **Subs Not Used:** McGregor, Boyd, Steven Fletcher, Berra.

SCOTLAND 0 NORWAY 0

It was a debut to forget for Wolves' striker Chris Iwelumo, whose unbelievable miss meant Scotland came away with a 0-0 draw with Norway at Hampden.

The result was all the more frustrating for the Tartan Army given that the Norwegians were perceived to be under-strength, and fielded a debutant goalkeeper in Jon Knudsen.

One man Scotland defenders did not like to see facing them was Aston Villa's John Carew, who gave the defence a torrid time all afternoon. In the early stages only a combined block from Gary Caldwell and Gary Naysmith stopped the physical striker from having an opening.

After Carew once more got the better of the home defence Craig Gordon was able to stop his effort, and Bjorn Helge Riise lacked composure as he blasted the rebound over.

→

James Morrison had Scotland's best chance of the first half, but even that was not clear-cut, and after the interval it was back to the norm, as Carew again forced Gordon into action.

On the hour George Burley made a double substitution when he sent on Iwelumo and Steven Fletcher and, within minutes, Iwelumo had his head in his hands.

Naysmith found the debutant at the back post three yards out but, inexplicably, his right-foot shot flew wide when it was easier to score.

A few chances did fall for either side, with Kjetil Waehler hitting a post, but in the end a draw was about the fairest result.

SCOTLAND: Gordon, Broadfoot, Weir, Caldwell, Naysmith, Brown, Darren Fletcher, Robson, Morrison (Steven Fletcher 56), McFadden (Iwelumo 57), Maloney.
Subs Not Used: McGregor, Alexander, Boyd, Hartley, Berra.

NORWAY: Knudsen, Hoiland, Waehler, Hangeland, John Arne Riise, Bjorn Helge Riise (Braaten 56), Stromstad (Pedersen 76), Grindheim, Winsnes, Iversen, Carew.
Subs Not Used: Jarstein, Skjonsberg, Elyounossi, Haestad, Haland.

HOLLAND 3 SCOTLAND 0

Scotland were beaten 3-0 at the Amsterdam ArenA by a rampant Dutch side who maintained their 100% record in Group Nine

The result may have been different had Kenny Miller taken an early chance but Joris Mathijsen was able to get back to block.

Despite having by far the bulk of the possession, only the skills of Arjen Robben stood out and so it came as somewhat of a surprise when Holland took the lead on the half hour.

Slack marking in the visiting defence allowed Klaas Jan Huntelaar space at the back post to meet Mark van Bommel's cross from deep, and the Real Madrid man guided his header into the net.

It was 2-0 just before the interval, when Robin van Persie escaped the attentions of Darren Fletcher to head in from close range.

Just after the break it was almost out of sight for Scotland. More good work from Robben set up Dirk Kuyt to drag a shot wide, then Robben himself could have got on the scoresheet but he snatched at the ball and let Scotland off the hook.

It looked like the visitors had found an unlikely way back into the match, when Gary Caldwell headed home a Ross McCormack free-kick. The celebrations were not to last when referee Laurent Duhamel ruled that Maarten Stekelenburg had been fouled, which looked a very harsh decision.

The scoring was completed 12 minutes from time when Kuyt converted from the spot after Christophe Berra had fouled Huntelaar in the area.

HOLLAND: Stekelenburg, van der Wiel, Mathijsen, Ooijer, van Bronckhorst, Kuyt, van Bommel, De Jong (Schaars 80), Robben, Huntelaar (Afellay 80), van Persie (Sneijder 65). **Subs Not Used:** Timmer, Boulahrouz, Braafheid, van der Vaart.

SCOTLAND: McGregor, Alexander (Hutton 73), Berra, Caldwell, Naysmith, Brown, Darren Fletcher, Ferguson, McCormack, Teale (Morrison 85), Miller (Steven Fletcher 71). **Subs Not Used:** Gordon, Barr, Iwelumo, Rae.

SCOTLAND 2 ICELAND 1

Scotland once again got back to winning ways with a 2-1 victory over Iceland at Hampden, and much like the previous game in Reykjavik, the game was never comfortable for the Scots.

Scotland began to press but could only create half chances for both Darren and Steven Fletcher, as the three-match quest for a home goal at Hampden showed no sign of ending. End it did, six minutes before the break through Cardiff City striker Ross McCormack.

The pace and power of Alan Hutton down the right helped him to get past a couple of Icelandic defenders, and when he cut the ball back across goal, McCormack was on hand to fire a first-time shot high into the net for the opener.

Into the second half and it was still right-back Hutton who was Scotland's biggest attacking threat. The Spurs man volleyed wide from distance, then after a neat exchange of passes, drilled a powerful shot that Gunnleifur Gunnleifsson saved well.

Iceland found a way back into the match in the 54th minute, when Palmi Palmason's spectacular strike clattered off the upright and Indridi Sigurdsson reacted well to dispatch the rebound into the net.

The visitors were not level for long however, as Steven Fletcher grabbed his first international goal to restore Scotland's lead 10 minutes later, heading Stephen McManus' knock-down past Gunnleifsson.

James Morrison had a couple of chances to wrap things up with the game drawing to a close, but it took a great double save by Craig Gordon to make sure of the points as Iceland sought an unlikely late leveller.

SCOTLAND: Gordon, Hutton, McManus, Caldwell, Naysmith, Morrison (Rae 90), Darren Fletcher, Brown, McCormack, Miller, Steven Fletcher (Teale 78). **Subs Not Used:** McGregor, Berra, Ferguson, Clarkson, Whittaker.

ICELAND: Gunnleifsson, Danielsson, Kristjan Orn Sigurdsson, Indridi Sigurdsson (Bjornsson 80), Eiriksson, Steinsson, Aron Gunnarsson (Eggert Jonsson 70), Helguson, Palmason, Gudjohnsen, Smarason. **Subs Not Used:** Arason, Gudmundsson, Ragnar Sigurdsson, Gunnarson, Bjarnason.

INSTANT RECALL

1   WHO SCORED SCOTLAND'S GOALS IN THE 2-1 WIN OVER ICELAND IN THE WORLD CUP QUALIFIER AT HAMPDEN PARK LAST APRIL?

2   HOW MANY HIBS OR FORMER HIBS PLAYERS WERE IN THE SCOTLAND TEAM THAT NIGHT?

3   WHO PLAYED IN GOAL FOR SCOTLAND WHEN THEY FACED DIEGO MARADONA'S ARGENTINA AT HAMPDEN IN NOVEMBER 2008?

4   WHO CAPTAINED SCOTLAND AGAINST NORWAY IN THE WORLD CUP QUALIFIER AT HAMPDEN IN OCTOBER 2008?

5   WHO SCORED SCOTLAND'S GOALS IN THE 2-1 WIN OVER ICELAND IN THE WORLD CUP QUALIFIER IN REYKJAVIK?

6   IN WHICH CITY DID SCOTLAND OPEN THEIR 2010 WORLD CUP QUALIFYING GROUP?

7   WHAT WAS THE SCORE WHEN SCOTLAND FACED NORTHERN IRELAND IN A FRIENDLY MATCH AT HAMPDEN IN AUGUST 2008?

8   WHICH PLAYER MADE HIS INTERNATIONAL RETURN FOR SCOTLAND IN THAT MATCH AGAINST THE IRISH AFTER A SIX-YEAR ABSENCE?

9   WHICH TWO PLAYERS WON THEIR FIRST SCOTLAND CAPS IN THE SAME MATCH?

10 WHO DID SCOTLAND FACE IN GEORGE BURLEY'S FIRST MATCH IN CHARGE OF THE NATIONAL SIDE?

11 WHO SCORED SCOTLAND'S FIRST GOAL OF THE BURLEY ERA?

12 WHO HAD SCOTLAND'S FIRST CLEAN SHEET UNDER GEORGE BURLEY?

13 TRUE OR FALSE - SCOTLAND LOST 3-0 TO THE NETHERLANDS IN A 2010 WORLD CUP QUALIFYING MATCH IN ROTTERDAM.

14 WHO DID SCOTT BROWN WIN HIS FIRST SCOTLAND CAP AGAINST?

15 WHICH MANAGER GAVE CRAIG GORDON HIS FIRST INTERNATIONAL CAP?

16 WHERE DID DARREN FLETCHER MAKE HIS INTERNATIONAL DEBUT?

17 WHO DID KENNY MILLER SCORE HIS FIRST INTERNATIONAL GOAL AGAINST?

18 HOW MANY TIMES HAVE SCOTLAND PLAYED IN THE FINALS OF THE EUROPEAN CHAMPIONSHIPS?

19 WHO SCORED FROM THE PENALTY SPOT WHEN SCOTLAND BEAT THE FAROES 6-0 IN 2006?

20 WHO DID ROSS MCCORMACK MAKE HIS SCOTLAND DEBUT AGAINST?

ANSWERS ON PAGE 61

```
D O C H E R T Y G D
X B U R L E Y B F S
P B J O T F D A E M
B U D X J S M O R I
E S U B S T A R G T
A B X U J E C M U H
T Y T R K I L O S D
T M S G I N E N O L
I G Z H A T O D N L
E P X V S R D F I T
```

Find these Scotland Managers in the word-search
(names can go diagonal, vertical, horizontal or backwards):

1. Stein
2. Ferguson
3. Busby
4. Roxburgh
5. Ormond

6. Beattie
7. Docherty
8. MacLeod
9. Smith
10. Burley

ANSWERS ON PAGE 61

SCOTLAND

HERE WE LOOK AT SOME OF THE PLAYERS WHO HAVE WORN THE DARK BLUE WITH DISTINCTION. ALL HAD A PART TO PLAY IN SCOTLAND'S RICH FOOTBALL HISTORY.

SCOTLAND GREATS

Alan Morton

Caps: 31

Born in 1893, Alan Morton went on to make a significant mark on Scottish football in the first half of the 20th century. Nicknamed the "Wee Blue Devil", his wing play terrorised defences both at club and international level and was one of the "Wembley Wizards" who dismantled England in 1928.

Standing just 5'4", he started out at an amateur with Queen's Park and it was as an amateur that he made his international debut for Scotland in a 1-1 draw with Wales in Cardiff in the Home International Championship in February 1920 and he kept his place on the left wing for the match against Northern Ireland the following month which Scotland won 3-0 with Morton netting his first international goal.

The following year, by which time he had joined Rangers as legendary manager Bill Struth's first signing, he played and scored in a 3-0 win over England in front of 85,000 spectators at Hampden Park.
He was to win 31 caps for Scotland – at a time when there were significantly fewer international games – between 1920 to 1932, his last appearance in the dark blue being in a 3-1 win over France in Paris.
Morton particularly relished playing against the "Auld Enemy" and played in every fixture between the two nations between 1921-1932 with the exception of the 1926 clash at Old Trafford. His performance in the 5-1 1928 win at Wembley ensured a lasting place in the history of the international team as he tormented the England defence and laid on three goals for Alex Jackson.
At club level, he was also hugely admired as he played 13 years at Ibrox and made 495 appearances, scoring 115 goals. He made his debut against Airdrie in 1920 and, coincidentally, also played his last match against the same opposition. He played a big part in Rangers' 4-0 Scottish Cup final win over Celtic in 1928 when the trophy returned to Ibrox after a 25-year absence. Morton was later appointed to the Rangers' board of directors, the first former player to have been accorded such an honour and remained there until he died in 1971.

Jim Baxter

Caps: 34

Jim Baxter is remembered as one of the greatest players to have worn the dark blue and he was a big star on both sides of the border.

He started out at Raith Rovers but it was not long before Rangers spotted his potential and paid a then Scottish record transfer fee of £17,500 to take the 20 year-old to Ibrox in 1960. He spent five years with the club before heading to Sunderland for a couple of years and then on to Nottingham Forest before returning to Rangers briefly in 1969. A year later, he retired at the age of just 30 and having won 34 international caps for Scotland.

He will be remembered for his display of "keepie-uppie" at Wembley in 1967 where Scotland became the first team to defeat world champions England and it was a show of defiance after Scotland never qualified for the final stages the previous year. Always a showman, Baxter had extravagant skills and could swing a game single-handedly. He made his Scotland debut in November 1960 in a 5-2 win over Northern Ireland and his first goals came when he hit a double in a 3-2 defeat by Uruguay in a friendly match in 1962.

But he made a more telling impact against England at Wembley in 1963 when Scotland had to play for much of the match with ten men after Eric Caldow suffered a broken leg and there were no substitutes at the time. Baxter put Scotland ahead and two minutes later made it 2-0 from the penalty spot as he took over Caldow's duties and later confessed it was the first penalty kick he had taken. It gave Scotland some revenge for the 9-3 mauling they had received in the corresponding fixture two years previously and Baxter led the team in a lap of honour after the game. The player went on to captain his country on several occasions and he was fiercely proud of putting on the dark blue.

He captained the team that famously beat Italy 1-0 at Hampden in 1965 in a World Cup qualifier but playing in the finals of a major championship was to elude Baxter in spite of the fact Scotland had one of their most talented teams during his era. He died in 2001 after a long battle against cancer.

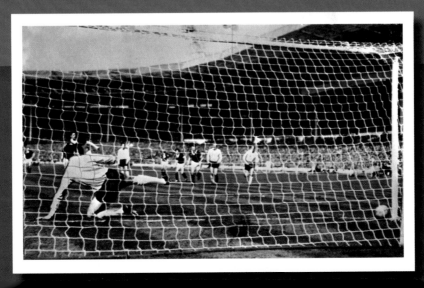

Denis Law

Caps: 55

Born in Aberdeen, Law's career began at Huddersfield Town in 1956 where he soon started to show his goal instinct as a raw teenager. Manchester City paid a British record £55,000 for his services but he spent only one season at Maine Road in his first spell as he then joined Italian side Torino for £110,000 – a record transfer between an English and Italian club.

But he did not settle and a year later was back in Manchester, this time signing for Matt Busby at United after they paid Torino £115,000 for his services. He went on to score 236 goals in 409 matches for the Old Trafford club and was a firm fans' favourite.

He is the only Scot to have won the European Footballer of the Year award – in 1964 – and scored 46 goals in one season, still a United club record. He was selected for the Rest of the World team for a match against England at Wembley where he scored in a 2-1 defeat. A knee injury meant he missed United's 1968 European Cup triumph over Benfica at Wembley.

He finished his playing career at Manchester City in 1974 where his final match was against Manchester United at Old Trafford where he scored a back-heel goal that contributed to his former team's relegation from the top flight.

At international level, Law was not selected for the 1958 World Cup finals in Sweden as he was still making his mark in the game but he made his Scotland debut later that year when he scored in a 3-0 win over Wales at Ninian Park.

He showed his worth when he scored twice in a 3-2 win over Czechoslovakia in a World Cup qualifier at Hampden in 1961 (although Scotland were to miss out on a place after losing a play-off to the Czechs in Belgium a couple of months later).

He scored four goals in a 5-1 win over Northern Ireland in 1962 and four in a 6-1 win over Norway the following year. He scored in the famous 3-2 win over England at Wembley in 1967.

Law finally had his chance to go to a World Cup at the end of his career in 1974 where he won his 55th and final cap in the 2-0 opening win over Zaire. He shares the international scoring record (30 goals) with Kenny Dalglish but his return is the more remarkable having come in just 55 matches.

Billy Bremner

Caps: 54

Born in Stirling, Billy Bremner – like Denis Law and Joe Jordan – left Scotland at an early age to pursue his football dreams south of the border. He made his Leeds United debut in 1960 and went on to play 770 games (scoring 115 goals) for the club.

The flame-haired right-half epitomised the qualities of Don Revie's Leeds and was tigerish in the tackle, strong in possession and could pass the ball with precision. He helped the club to the Second Division title in 1964 and then to the brink of the league and cup double the following season.

He took over the club captaincy from fellow-Scot Bobby Collins in 1966 and led Leeds through the most successful spell in their history. He captained them to the European Fairs' Cup (the forerunner of the UEFA Cup) in 1968 and 1971 and the League Championship in 1969 and 1974. Bremner played in four FA Cup finals for the club but was only on the winning side once (in 1972 in the Centenary final against Arsenal). He was voted Footballer of the Year in England in 1970. He had a knack of scoring crucial goals for the club but Leeds also had a habit of finishing runners-up and, as well as three FA Cup finals during Bremner's term, they were pipped for the league title on more than one occasion and lost in the finals of the European Cup-Winners' Cup (in 1973) and the European Cup (1975). After leaving Leeds, he had spells at Hull City and Doncaster Rovers before retiring from the game at the age of 39. He had management spells at all three clubs he played for. At international level, Bremner made his Scotland debut against Spain in a 0-0 draw at Hampden in May 1965 in a team that also included Billy McNeill, John Greig and Denis Law. He also played in the famous 3-2 win over England at Wembley two years later and became an automatic selection for his country. He captained the Scotland team for the 1974 World Cup finals in West Germany but had an agonising miss in the 0-0 draw with Brazil.

He went on to play 54 matches for Scotland and scored three goals including the winner against Austria in a World Cup qualifying match at Hampden in 1968. His other goals came in a 5-3 win over Wales in the Home International Championship at Wrexham the following year and against Spain in a European Championship qualifier in 1974.

He is included in both the Scottish and English Halls of Fame for his service to the game and he died at the age of 54 from a heart attack. Leeds erected a statue outside Elland Road as a tribute to his contribution to the club's history.

SCOTLAND GREATS

Joe Jordan

Caps: 52

Joe Jordan has the unique distinction of scoring for Scotland at three different World Cup finals and he has a special place in the affection of the Tartan Army. Not least because he headed the goal that beat Czechoslovakia at Hampden in 1973 to send Scotland to their first World Cup finals for 16 years. He went on to score the clinching goal against Zaire in West Germany in the 2-0 win that opened Scotland's finals campaign and also netted a late goal in the 1-1 draw with Yugoslavia which proved to no avail as Scotland missed out on qualifying for the later stages on goal difference.

When Scotland played in the 1978 finals in Argentina, he scored in the 3-1 defeat by Peru and, four years later in Spain, was also on target in a 2-2 draw against the USSR when Scotland also required a win to progress.

Born in Carluke, Jordan started out at Morton but his potential was soon spotted and Leeds United paid £15,000 to lure him south in 1970. That Leeds team under Don Revie scaled the heights of English and indeed European football and Jordan took his place at Elland Road alongside fellow Scots Billy Bremner and Eddie Gray.

He struggled to get into the starting eleven initially with Allan Clarke and Mick Jones forming a productive partnership as twin strikers but he later became a mainstay. He played for Leeds in two European finals – in the Cup-Winners' Cup in 1973 and in the European Cup in 1975 but on both occasions ended up on the losing side.

He was transferred to Manchester United in 1978 for £350,000 and spent three years at Old Trafford before signing for AC Milan in Italy where he enhanced his reputation as a whole-hearted striker.

He made his Scotland debut at Wembley in 1973 when he came on as a substitute in a 1-0 defeat by England but came off the bench to more devastating effect a few months later when he scored his first Scotland goal to sink Czechoslovakia in the World Cup qualifying tie at Hampden. Jordan went on to claim 11 goals for his country.

Kenny Dalglish

Caps: 102

Kenny Dalglish's cap record for Scotland looks set to stand for a good few years yet. First picked by Tommy Docherty for a European Championship qualifier against Belgium in 1971 when he came on as a substitute, Dalglish was a Scotland regular for 15 years.

He made his name playing under Jock Stein at Celtic where he made over 200 appearances and averaged a goal every second game before heading south to join Liverpool for a then record £440,000 as a replacement for Kevin Keegan in 1977. Dalglish took his career to new heights and scored the winning goal against Bruges in the European Cup final in 1978 at Wembley and was an integral part of the successful Liverpool team which swept all before them in the late 1970s, early 1980s.

He formed a formidable scoring partnership with Ian Rush at Anfield and became the first player to score 100 goals in both the Scottish and English League.

At international level, Willie Ormond selected him for the 1974 World Cup finals in West Germany where he played in all three matches (against Zaire, Brazil and Yugoslavia) and he went on to play in Argentina in 1978 (again playing in all three matches), Spain 1982 and in Mexico in 1986.

He punctuated his Scotland career with some memorable goals – one through Ray Clemence's legs against England, and unforgettable solo goals against Belgium and Spain stand out.

He won his 102nd and final cap in a European Championship qualifying match against Luxembourg at Hampden in November 1986 and scored 30 goals for his country (equalling Denis Law's record). Dalglish went on to become a successful manager and had the rare distinction of guiding two different clubs (Liverpool and Blackburn) to the English League title. He was awarded an MBE for his services to the game.

SCOTLAND GREATS

Alex McLeish

Caps: 77

Only Kenny Dalglish and Jim Leighton have won more international caps and McLeish's Scotland career spanned 13 years, all while playing for Aberdeen at club level. He won his first cap in 1980 in a European Championship qualifier against Portugal at Hampden alongside Alan Hansen in central defence in a 4-1 victory and became an automatic first choice, more often than not alongside club-mate Willie Miller.

A rock at the heart of the defence, he helped Aberdeen to three Scottish Premier League titles and five Scottish Cup triumphs and, most famously, to the European Cup-Winners' Cup in Gothenburg in 1983 with a win over the mighty Real Madrid. Alex Ferguson was a huge influence on him as a player and it extended after he retired as McLeish went on to manage the international team.

As a player, McLeish played at three World Cup finals – coming on as a late substitute against Brazil in a 4-1 defeat in Seville in 1982 and then also playing against Denmark in Mexico four years later and played in all three games in Italy in 1990. He won his final international cap when he captained Scotland in a 3-0 win over Malta in a World Cup qualifier at Ibrox in 1993.

He went on to captain Aberdeen and was voted Scottish Footballer of the Year in 1990 but resisted any temptation to move south with Tottenham Hotspur and Manchester United both linked with him at different stages in his career.

After he hung up his boots, he went into management, firstly with Motherwell and later at Hibernian and then Rangers where he guided the Ibrox side to two Premier League titles.

After leaving Ibrox to make way for the brief Paul Le Guen era, he went on to take over the reins of the international team when Walter Smith returned to Ibrox as manager. McLeish achieved a famous 1-0 win over France in Paris as Scotland put themselves in a great position to qualify for Euro 2008 but the heartbreaking defeat by Italy in the final qualifying match at Hampden proved to be his last as Scotland manager. He proved to be, statistically, Scotland's most successful manager with a 70 per cent win record.

SCOTLAND GREATS

Gary McAllister

Caps: 57

Gary McAllister started out with his local side Motherwell but went on to achieve greatness in England and is fondly remembered by fans of Leeds United and Liverpool as well as the Tartan Army.

He moved from Motherwell to Leicester City at the age of 20 but it was when he signed for Leeds in 1990 in a £1 million deal that his career began to blossom. The club had just won promotion to the top flight and finished a respectable fourth in that first season. Two years later, a team built around the midfield quartet of Gordon Strachan, McAllister, David Batty and Gary Speed won the league title. McAllister spent six seasons at Elland Road and captained the team at the 1996 League Cup final against Aston Villa at Wembley but it ended in a 3-0 defeat. He played 294 games and scored 45 goals before joining Coventry City in a £3 million deal and then enjoyed an "Indian Summer" to his career when he was a surprise signing at Liverpool at the age of 35 in 2000.

He went on to help them gain Champions League qualification in that first season and also win the FA Cup when he came on as a substitute to turn the tide against Arsenal. McAllister sent Liverpool into the UEFA Cup final by scoring from the penalty spot against Barcelona and then played his part in the remarkable 5-4 win over Deportivo Alaves in the final in Germany. He scored another penalty but had a hand in three of the other goals and was later named "Man of the Match" being awarded an MBE in 2001. He rejoined Coventry as player-manager in 2002 and took over as Leeds United manager in early 2008.

For Scotland, he made his debut against East Germany in a 1-0 friendly defeat at Hampden in April 1990 and netted his first goal for his country in a 2-1 European Championship qualifying win in the October. It helped Andy Roxburgh's side qualify for the final stages of a European Championship for the first time and McAllister scored from the penalty spot in the final 3-0 win over the CIS in Sweden but, by that stage, narrow defeats at the hands of Holland and Germany had left Scotland short of progressing.

By the start of Scotland's next European Championship qualifying campaign, McAllister was captaining the team and he helped Scotland progress to another finals, this time in England. After a 0-0 draw with Holland, Scotland lost painfully to England with McAllister seeing a second-half penalty saved by David Seaman as Scotland again missed out on the latter stages. McAllister won his final cap in March 1999 in a 2-1 European Championship qualifier defeat by the Czech Republic at Celtic Park.

HOW MUCH CAN YOU REMEMBER ABOUT SCOTLAND'S PAST? TAKE OUR SHORT QUIZ TO SEE HOW YOU MEASURE UP

1. WHO WON THE MOST CAPS – JIM LEIGHTON, ALEX MCLEISH OR WILLIE MILLER?

2. WHO WAS THE FIRST SCOTLAND PLAYER TO WIN 50 CAPS?

3. WHO WAS COLIN HENDRY'S LAST SCOTLAND GAME AGAINST?

4. HOW MANY GOALS DID ALLY MCCOIST SCORE FOR HIS COUNTRY IN 61 APPEARANCES?

5. WHO WAS THE RANGERS' STRIKER WHO NETTED FOUR GOALS FOR SCOTLAND IN A WORLD CUP QUALIFIER IN 1969?

6. HOW MANY CELTIC PLAYERS PLAYED IN THE FAMOUS 3-2 WIN OVER ENGLAND AT WEMBLEY IN 1967?

7. WHAT WAS THE SCORE WHEN SCOTLAND PLAYED ENGLAND AT FIRST HAMPDEN PARK IN 1878?

8. HOW LONG WAS ALLY MACLEOD SCOTLAND MANAGER?

9. WHO WAS SCOTLAND MANAGER BEFORE ANDY ROXBURGH?

10. OF THE GREAT OLD FIRM CAPTAINS JOHN GREIG AND BILLY MCNEILL – WHO WAS CAPPED MORE TIMES FOR SCOTLAND?

11. WHO SCORED SCOTLAND'S LAST GOAL AT A WORLD CUP FINALS?

12. HOW MANY MATCHES HAVE SCOTLAND WON IN EUROPEAN CHAMPIONSHIP FINALS?

13. WHO SCORED SCOTLAND'S LAST GOAL AT A EUROPEAN CHAMPIONSHIP FINALS?

14. WHO SCORED SCOTLAND'S WINNING GOAL IN A FAMOUS FRIENDLY VICTORY OVER ARGENTINA AT HAMPDEN IN 1990?

15. WHICH OF THE SPL MANAGERS IN THE 2008-09 SEASON HAS SCORED THE MOST INTERNATIONAL GOALS?

16. WHO DID KENNY DALGLISH WIN MORE CAPS PLAYING FOR – CELTIC OR LIVERPOOL?

17. WHAT WAS SCOTLAND'S BIGGEST-EVER WIN?

18. WHAT HAS BEEN SCOTLAND'S BIGGEST-EVER DEFEAT?

19. WHAT MILESTONE DID MAURICE JOHNSTON ACHIEVE WHEN HE PLAYED AGAINST YUGOSLAVIA IN OCTOBER 1988?

20. WHO WAS SCOTLAND MANAGER WHEN THEY QUALIFIED FOR THE 1974 WORLD CUP FINALS IN WEST GERMANY?

ANSWERS ON PAGE 61

```
B L M R Q B F H G V P
Q R M C K F S M R P A
W R E C G D Q B E L F
O E I M L R Q X I A Y
L A M O N E A F G I O
D H H C C E I I N T U
F T O E N H R S N K N
S R G N N E H I H E G
P M E L T D I C T N L
N E P A L U R L Z S G
S O U N E S S Y L B T
```

Find these Scotland Captains in the word-search
(names can go diagonal, vertical, horizontal or backwards) :

1. Young
2. Bremner
3. Aitken
4. Souness
5. Greig
6. McLeish
7. Hendry
8. McGrain
9. Rioch
10. McNeill

THE NEXT BATCH - BILLY STARK

AS SCOTTISH FA NATIONAL YOUTH TEAMS' COACH, BILLY STARK IS BETTER PLACED THAN ANYONE TO REVEAL WHAT COACHES ARE LOOKING FOR IN YOUNG PLAYERS. HERE, HE GIVES US HIS EXCLUSIVE THOUGHTS ON WHAT PLAYERS HAVE TO STRIVE FOR.

1 LOVE THE GAME - The first thing for a young player is to foster a love for the game. Nowadays, with all the television exposure that football gets, it certainly attracts children. A love for playing the game has to be there. You have to be prepared to go and practise in all weathers with a ball. We see the finished product in the Champions League and the English Premiership and I think we all aspire to that. But it's a long, long road to get there and there are a lot of things needed to get there.

2 PRACTISE, PRACTISE, PRACTISE - The players at the top still practise but it is when you are young that you form the fundamental skills which make you a player.
In my day, if there was nothing doing then you'd go out and kick the ball against a wall; it was just the way it was then. Of course, we understand that there are so many different things to do now and it's almost a case of weaning themselves off the other things.
Everyone has different circumstances and if you have access to all these things, then the normal child would be quite happy to use them. But the more time spent with a ball, the better in order to enjoy practising. Children have better facilities now and I think they expect that - and certainly the parents do - whereas in the past you'd play in the street.
That was the good old days in producing loads of players because everyone was playing football every single day. If children can find the time, they should practise.

3 GET A BALANCE - If you're left-sided, you have a head start on others because there is a scarcity of that type of player even nowadays.
A manager in his best-case scenario is looking for a balance about his team and you'll still get a lot of left-sided centre-backs who are right-footed and even full-backs and midfield players on the left side who are right-footed.
So, it's good to work on both feet but obviously you have to master your good foot and get that to work and then that's the time to work with your weaker foot.

4 TACTICS - It is all about players, after all, and if I have 11 superior players and if you come up with a good set of tactics to stop us playing, we have an off-day and your guys have a good day, then you can win.
But more often than not, 11 good players - if their appetite is right - are going to win the game. The bottom-line is about players and not tactics and I don't think youngsters need to worry about that side of the game when they are developing.
Because of the whole television product, the game is analysed and dissected. That can increase your knowledge of the game but I think it's mastery of the ball that is the first thing you must have.

5 POSITIONING - At a young age, if you are big then normally you play centre-half and that's the stereotyping we have. But I think if you can play in different positions at an early age, then I think that's better. When you played in the street, you didn't have positions and that's how you honed your skills.
There are different stages when you can learn about team positions but the main thing is to spend as much time with the ball as you possibly can.

THE NEXT BATCH - BILLY STARK

6 FITNESS - Nowadays, the game is so athletically-based that sometimes the football side is lost. If you get to any level at all, your training will ensure that you are at the required fitness level to play. But there are a lot of things come into fitness at the top level. You can lose a lot through nervous energy and there is a confidence thing about it.

You can reach a good standard of fitness but you also have to be able to handle everything that goes with playing in a big game and not losing it through nerves. Sometimes it can work the other way where you can be driven on by adrenaline.

7 PACE - Coaches can maybe improve a player's speed slightly but they can't turn someone who's not quick into a speed merchant. There are examples of players down through the years who were maybe good at other sports but once you get to a certain age, you make a choice. Some players need to play other sports to keep developing. I recently read an article about top tennis players who are playing football in an attempt to give them quick feet to get about the tennis court. Playing other sports can give you an edge and also improve fitness but each sport has its own specifics in terms of training and football is no different. There are examples of players who have crossed into other sports with great success.

8 DIET - Sometimes it's hard to control those things as it's down to how the parents bring them up but I'd say nowadays children who want to play football are far more aware of their diets as you see them with their sports drinks and energy bars. I don't think there's much to educate there - they are pretty good that way and far better than we were when we were growing up.

9 DESIRE - You need a desire and hunger to be a footballer and realise that you have to make sacrifices. The rewards of the game nowadays should certainly be incentive enough for young players. They need to be determined, learn how to deal with setbacks and there can be a fine line between making the grade and not making the grade and luck can play a part as well. You can be having a good spell and someone sees you and wants to sign you and you go on from there. Coaches can spot ability. You don't necessarily need to have had a good game but they can spot other qualities in a player such as desire and willingness to work hard on the pitch. There is no way you can carry passengers now. Even if you are the best player in the team, you can't just stroll about until you get the ball.

10 SIZE - The British game is based on power and pace. But it's too easy to generalise and say that players don't make it because of their size. Generally, the ones that make it are the ones that want it badly enough and, in terms of physique, it shouldn't necessarily come into it. Even at international level, when you come up against the French, Germans or Italians, they are big, athletic players but they often have smaller players and you can bet they are special players if they can make it in that company. There is room for players of all sizes and I don't think anyone should be downhearted and feel they should be six-foot plus and built like a middleweight boxer. There are loads of things that come into it and it's a case of working on your strengths and improving your weaknesses.

STARK CHOICES

Billy Stark looks at some emerging players to watch out for who have the potential to be future senior international players:

ALEX MacDONALD – The Burnley striker (currently on loan at Falkirk) has a terrific attitude to the game. Apart from his ability, he works really hard for the team - he's a team player. Small, compact, explosive type of player and I think he'll develop into a really good player.

JOHN FLECK - He's been the best player at every age-level and he's coped with that pressure. He has superb poise and composure and has a maturity well beyond his years. For a 17 year-old to get through to the Rangers first-team shows how good he is. He has a lovely left foot - I'm not sure what his best position is going to be - but he has a lovely range of passing and is able to do something a bit different in games.

JAMES FORREST - He was spotted quite late and he was 16 when Celtic took him. He's a winger who has a surge of explosive pace and that type of player is quite thin on the ground and I'm hopeful he will develop. He has another year in the Under-19s so he has time to develop.

PAUL HANLON - He's made his way into the first-team at Hibs. He's going to be a really good centre-half. He's been used at left-back but he's played already for the Scotland Under-21s which shows how much potential he has.

CALLUM BOOTH – He is another who has been doing well in the Hibs' Under-19 team. He's a big, rangy player who is a good attacking full-back. He has plenty of natural ability.

A LOOK BACK AT FIVE OF SCOTLAND'S GREATEST GAMES AND HOW WE HAVE HELD OUR OWN AGAINST THE GREATS OF WORLD FOOTBALL.

NOVEMBER 9, 1965
WORLD CUP QUALIFIER
SCOTLAND 1 ITALY 0

Scotland needed a victory to keep their hopes alive of qualifying for the 1966 World Cup finals in England. A 2-1 home defeat to Poland a month earlier – when the Poles scored twice in the final six minutes – meant Scotland had to raise their game considerably to face the Italians. Italy named a strong line-up which included Giacinto Facchetti, Alessandro Mazzola and Gianni Rivera and a crowd of 100,393 filled Hampden more in hope than expectation.

It was a match of few chances. Mazzola came close with a shot across the face of goal but Neil Martin had a chance at the other end only to send his shot into the side-netting.

Willie Henderson opened up the Italian defence on several occasions but Scotland could not find the finishing touch in front of goal. Mazzola had another opportunity late on for Italy but lost control at the vital time. With just two minutes left, Scotland won it with a goal from the unlikely boot of John Greig.

The Rangers defender had been deployed at right-back but he surged forward in the closing moments. He took a pass from Billy Bremner, fed Jim Baxter and then raced onto the return pass to drill a low left-foot shot past William Negri from the edge of the area.

The "Hampden Roar" greeted the goal that kept World Cup hopes alive. But the following month Italy beat them 3-0 in Naples to end any hopes of playing in the finals.

JUNE 18, 1974
WORLD CUP FINALS, GERMANY
BRAZIL 0 SCOTLAND 0

The Waldstadion in Frankfurt was almost packed to capacity with 60,000 fans squeezing in to see if Scotland could upset the world champions after beating Zaire 2-0 in their opening group match.

Admittedly, the Brazilian team of 1974 was re-cast from the 1970 model which can lay claim to being one of the best teams in the history of the game. But Jairzinho, top scorer in 1970, and Rivelino, who could still bend a free-kick or two into the top corner of the net, were still around.

If the flair was not what it was, it should be remembered that this team went on to lose narrowly to Holland in what was effectively the semi-final of the competition and eventually finished fourth after losing 1-0 to Poland in the 3rd-4th play-off.

Scotland knew that a win would virtually put them through to the second phase and battled Brazil all the way.m Leivinha provided an early scare when he hit the crossbar from a corner from Nelinho but David Harvey would have expected a busier 90 minutes. Scotland had their chances too and Davie Hay had a dominant match in midfield and forced a terrific save from Leao with a long-range effort.
But it was Billy Bremner who came closest to a goal when the ball rebounded off his shins in a crowded penalty area as he stood just a couple of yards out and was unable to divert it into a gaping net.

The draw was still a significant result for Willie Ormond's side and it meant their hopes of reaching the next stage were still alive. A 1-1 draw with Yugoslavia in their final match – while Brazil beat Zaire 3-0 – meant Scotland went out on goal difference, the first team to exit a World Cup without losing a match.

THANKS FOR THE MEMORIES

OCTOBER 7, 2006
**EUROPEAN CHAMPIONSHIP QUALIFIER
SCOTLAND 1 FRANCE 0**

Scotland moved to the top of Group B in their qualifying group for Euro 2008 with an unlikely win over France at Hampden. The Tartan Army celebrated one of Scotland's greatest results long into the night after Gary Caldwell had proved the match-winner. Scotland spent much of the 90 minutes with their backs to the wall and were glad to go in at half-time still on level terms.

Thierry Henry hit a post and Patrick Vieiri and David Trezeguet both put the ball in the net for France only for the linesman's flag to come to Scotland's rescue. Craig Gordon was the busier of the goalkeepers and pulled off a tremendous save shortly before half-time to deny Florent Malouda.

Walter Smith's team had to keep their discipline against the star-studded French team and there was some resolute defending as the Scots repelled wave after wave of attacks.

But France's frustrations were becoming apparent in the second half as Scotland grew in self-belief. James McFadden, playing as a lone striker, managed to get in behind the French defence on one occasion but the angle was tight and he could not get his effort on target.

But, after 67 minutes, Scotland made the breakthrough. A Paul Hartley corner found its way to Caldwell and he swept the ball low into the net to send Hampden wild with delight.

Scotland knew they would face a late onslaught as France tried to retrieve the situation but battened down the hatches and looked even more determined to hold on for a famous win.

Henry had a great chance to equalise with three minutes left when he was not picked up in the Scotland penalty area but his tame header was easily saved by Gordon and it was clear it was not going to be France's day. Overwhelming relief greeted the final whistle and Scotland emerged as genuine contenders for a place at Euro 2008.

THANKS FOR THE MEMORIES

NOVEMBER 14, 1984
WORLD CUP QUALIFIER
SCOTLAND 3 SPAIN 1

Scotland were seeking to reach their fourth successive World Cup finals but had endured a difficult time in their European Championship qualifying group in their previous campaign where they finished bottom behind Belgium, Switzerland and East Germany.

So Scotland went into their World Cup qualifying campaign under Jock Stein knowing it would be a difficult task to get through in a group that also included Spain and Wales.

Beating Iceland 3-0 in their opening match in Glasgow, the Scots knew that a win over the Spanish would set them up well in the group.

Spain came to Glasgow with a fantastic reputation, having reached the final of the European Championships a few months previously only to lose to Michel Platini's France. But Scotland went into the match with confidence and Stein named a strong side which included Willie Miller, Alex McLeish, Davie Cooper, Graeme Souness and Kenny Dalglish.

But it was Mo Johnston, who had signed for Celtic from Watford in the summer, who made his impact on the game with two well-taken goals in the first half to give Scotland a healthy half-time advantage. Spain came back in the second half and Andoni Goicoechea pulled a goal back in the 68th minute when he beat Jim Leighton to give them hope of pulling off a draw. Their hopes were extinguished seven minutes later.

This game will remembered for an exquisite solo goal from Dalglish with 15 minutes left as he waltzed through the Spanish defence before clipping the ball past Luis Arconada to settle the issue.

Scotland eventually finished second in the qualifying group but beat Australia in a two-leg play-off to book their place in the finals in Mexico.

NOVEMBER 15, 2003,
EUROPEAN CHAMPIONSHIP PLAY-OFF, FIRST LEG
SCOTLAND 1 HOLLAND 0

Scotland were drawn against Holland, ranked fifth in the world, over a two-leg Euro 2004 play-off.

Berti Vogts, who took Germany to the European title eight years previously, had signalled a new era for the international team after replacing Craig Brown. Scotland knew they had to take some sort of lead to Holland for the return and James McFadden scored what proved to be the only goal of the game after 20 minutes. He exchanged passes with Darren Fletcher before netting with the aid of a deflection to set Hampden alight.

Holland fought back and both Lee Wilkie and Gary Naysmith made goal-line clearances as Robert Douglas was put under serious pressure by the Dutch. The goalkeeper saved well from a header from Ruud van Nistelrooy and then there was a let-off for Scotland midway through the second half when Andy van der Meyde struck the crossbar with Douglas beaten. Scotland spent much of the game with their backs to the wall but defended stubbornly and kept Holland at bay.

Remarkably, it could have been 2-0 after 78 minutes when Stephen Pearson volleyed narrowly wide after good work from Kenny Miller. Holland also had chances in the closing moments but a combination of good defending and good luck meant it was a frustrating afternoon for them. Scotland held on for the win to keep their hopes of reaching Euro 2004 alive although there was the small matter of the return leg a few days later at the Amsterdam ArenA.

The Dutch took full revenge with a 6-0 mauling on a night which will go down as one

NO. 1 FANS

SPOTLIGHT on - THE FANS

PAUL ALLISON

YEARS IN TRAVEL/SCOTLAND SUPPORTERS CLUB:

I joined the STC in 1997 along with a fellow Scottish friend in Southampton - we were season ticket holders sat next to each other at The Dell (Southampton FC's old ground), and decided it was our duty to support the national side as well. We were both 21 at the time.

FIRST SCOTLAND MATCH AT HAMPDEN:

I started watching Scotland games at a time when Hampden was being renovated, so my first home game was against Latvia at Celtic Park. I didn't get to see Scotland at Hampden until the Lithuania home match in 1999.

MOST MEMORABLE TRIP:

This would probably be Moldova in 2004. Since learning some tourist Russian at night school, it was my aim to get to use it in a Russian-speaking country, so when this trip came up, I booked like a shot. We managed quite a lot of off-the-beaten-track sightseeing, including taking in a local league game the weekend after the Scotland match. Unfortunately the performance on the pitch was pretty poor as the team failed to hit the target in a 0-0 draw, and it was to be Berti Vogts' last game in charge as the media were gunning for him by this point. He did share an elevator with me back at the hotel after the game though!

ANDY COOK

**YEARS IN TRAVEL/SCOTLAND
SUPPORTERS CLUB: 20 YEARS**

First Scotland Match at Hampden:
Scotland v Yugoslavia 19 October 1988 1 -1

First Scotland Match Abroad:
France v Scotland 11 October 1989 Even though we lost 3 – 0 I was hooked on travelling to follow Scotland after that.

MOST MEMORABLE TRIP:

Slovenia v Scotland 12 October 2005 0 – 3. With 3 stunning goals securing all 3 points, this trip had it all. I even ended up on Slovenian national television commenting on Slovenian women, which did get me a spot of bother when I got home!

MOST MEMORABLE MATCH:

My return trip to the Parc De Princes in Paris was a lot more memorable with that famous 1- 0 win against France on the 12 September 2007. I remember when James McFadden's wonderful strike hit the back of the net there was a few seconds of silence around the ground as it sunk in that we had actually scored and taken the lead!

MOST MEMORABLE EXPERIENCE:

Ukraine v Scotland 11 October 2006. I have had so many memorable experiences following Scotland, a lot not suitable for print, but I'll always remember the trip to Kiev. I was involved with the Tartan Army Children's Charity whose goal is to bring a little happiness and support to disadvantaged children in Scotland and in countries in which Scotland play. I always have so much fun following Scotland so it's nice to be able to give something back. Over £10,000 was raised by fans and donated to the Kiev special school of arts for children with impaired vision and the Kiev City Orphanage (Pritulok) Number 5. Meeting the children and seeing what a difference our money would make is an experience I'll never forget

**ALL-TIME FAVOURITE
SCOTLAND PLAYER:**

Kenny Dalglish

NO. 1 FANS

ALLAN MACKILLOP

YEARS IN TRAVEL/SCOTLAND SUPPORTERS CLUB:

13, unlucky for some.

MOST MEMORABLE TRIP:

A couple actually – Bordeaux '98 for the atmosphere after the match and Slovenia for both the post-match atmosphere and the performance.

MOST MEMORABLE MATCH:

Both performances home and away against France during the last Euro qualifiers were great moments, especially the 1 – 0 win in Paris. One of those times when I was glad to say: "I wiz there."

MOST MEMORABLE EXPERIENCE:

Arriving at the Stade De France for the opening game of the 1998 World Cup on the back of an RAC recovery vehicle – the bus had broken down on the way to the stadium. Also, getting lifted bodily onto the ramparts of Ljubljana castle. I wasn't that fussy to see over the edge, honest!

ALL-TIME FAVOURITE SCOTLAND PLAYER:

Kenny Dalglish

JOHN MCFARLANE

YEARS IN TRAVEL/SCOTLAND SUPPORTERS CLUB

I joined the Scotland Travel Club in July 96 just after the European Championships in England and just before the beginning of the France 98 World Cup Campaign. I didn't miss a game home or away in the 98 qualifying campaign and managed to get a ticket for each of our 3 World Cup games in France. Great memories.

MOST MEMORABLE MATCH:

During the last decade or so we have had some memorable games st home and away.

Away from home we have beaten England at Wembley (if only Christian Dailly's header had gone in), beaten France in Paris. Who will ever forget James McFadden's wonder strike. At home we have experienced notable victories against Holland, France and Ukraine and drawn against Germany and Italy.

However my most memorable match for no other reason other than the significance of the occasion has to be the opening game of France 98. 10th June 1998 against Brazil at the Stade de France. I was fortunate enough to get a ticket for the game and arrived in Paris 2 days before the game. The atmosphere in the city prior to the game was fantastic. It was certainly spot the celebrity time, Ewan McGregor, Sir Sean, Rod Stewart etc. Everyone appeared to be in town to get behind the team. Most of the supporters appear to have made for the "Auld Alliance" and the streets arouwnd that particular hostelry were a sea of tartan and flags. I made it out to the ground around 2.30 which was 3 hours before kick off. It was great to see the players come on to the park and come over and wave to the supporters to who were seated behind one of the goals.

The World Cup opening ceremony began around 4.30 and the main event Scotland v Brazil at 5.30. We didn't get off to the best of starts with Sampaio scoring for Brazil after only 4 minutes. We gradually worked our way back into the game and we were awarded a penalty 7 minutes from half time. Super cool John Collins stroked the equaliser away. It was absolutely fantastic inside the stadium. I remember looking up at the scoreboard at half time Brazil - 1 Scotland 1. As everyone knows we eventually lost out 2-1 due to an unfortunate own goal by Tom Boyd.

It was a fantastic occasion and Scotland played well on the day. The support as usual were superb and gave the players a great reception when they came towards us at the end of the game. Great memories.

ALL-TIME FAVOURITE SCOTLAND PLAYER:

Kenneth Mathieson
Dalglish - King Kenny

SPOTLIGHT on - THE FANS

NO. 1 FANS

JENNIFER BLACKWOOD

**YEARS IN TRAVEL/SCOTLAND
SUPPORTERS CLUB: 6 years**

FIRST SCOTLAND MATCH AT HAMPDEN:

Technically a school boys' international back in the 70s but I don't remember much of it so the Scotland v Germany game in 2003 which ended in a one all draw.

MOST MEMORABLE TRIP:

Every trip is memorable for different reasons but Slovenia probably edges it - superb country, superb result, great atmosphere at the ground.... just a pity it didn't really count for anything as we were already out of the tournament.

MOST MEMORABLE MATCH:

Paris!! I don't think I stopped shaking from Faddy scoring until the end of the game. I kept getting texts through the match from people back home asking 'are you there? it must be amazing!'...it was!

MOST MEMORABLE EXPERIENCE:

Any of the Tartan Army Sunshine Appeal visits. We give a donation to a children's charity in every country that we visit. We visited children's cancer wards in Kiev, Bari and Milan, an orphanage in Moldova, Children's hospital in Estonia and much more.

ALL-TIME FAVOURITE SCOTLAND PLAYER:

Joe Jordan...his toothless smile is an iconic image!

IFEOMA DIEKE HAS SHOWN THAT IT IS POSSIBLE TO EARN A FULL-TIME LIVING IN WOMEN'S FOOTBALL. CAPPED MORE THAN 50 TIMES FOR SCOTLAND, SHE IS ENJOYING HER SECOND SPELL PLAYING PROFESSIONALLY IN AMERICA.

Ifeoma Dieke has shown that it is possible to earn a full-time living in women's football. Capped more than 50 times for Scotland, she is enjoying her second spell playing professionally in America.

Ifeoma Dieke has spent much of her life in America but there is no question where her allegiance lies.

Having won over 50 caps for Scotland, she would dearly love to go on and reach 100 like international team-mates Pauline Hamill and Julie Fleeting.

Yet the tough-tackling defender had the options of playing for three countries. Born in Massachusetts, she was approached by America but she also qualified for Nigeria, through her parents, Ken and Edith.

But, having moved to Scotland at the age of three and having been brought up in Cumbernauld, there was no question which shirt she would be pulling over her shoulders.

Her return to the States came when she won a soccer scholarship to Florida International University in Miami after being spotted playing for Cumbernauld and she has now carved out a professional career for herself with Chicago Red Stars in the new Women's Professional Soccer (WPS).

It is the second attempt to launch the professional women's game in America after the money dried up on the Women's United Soccer Association in 2003. The new league – which has just enjoyed its first season – covers the major

American cities - Washington, Los Angeles, Boston and New York also have teams - and three new sides (from Atlanta, Dallas and Philadelphia) come on stream in March.

Dieke, who played in the previous incarnation for Atlanta Beat, was the only Scot playing in the new set-up (where she came up against Julie Fleeting's San Diego Spirit on a couple of occasions) and has had the chance to draw comparisons.

"I don't think the money was spent very wisely in the WUSA. The budget was for five years and most of it was spent in the first two years so they ran into problems," the 28 year-old explains. "We knew the writing was on the wall when we were at Atlanta and we knew it could be that last year of the league.

"There were player meetings and conference calls and then they were looking to cut salaries by 25 per cent and even a big star like Mia Hamm - who was on a six-figure sum - faced a cut.

"I don't see the same mistakes being made again. The correct structure is in place this time and there is television coverage from the Fox Sports Channel which shows the English Premier League.

"It has a better chance this time. There will be a five-year gap since the last league ended and the new one begins and a lot of planning has gone into it." Dieke certainly enjoyed her return to the pro ranks in America. "Things started off really well for us and, in the first four games, we won two and drew two," she goes on. But then we lost three games

"The standard is what I expected – every game is competitive and the encounters are close and many games are decided by just the odd goal. "Every team showed they were capable of going on a run and it's been a good experience. Our attendances averaged 4,000 plus and we received good local media coverage.

"Nationally, the games were televised weekly and sometimes re-aired and there has been a good general interest in the league."

The success of the league has shown that there is an audience for the game out there and such was the interest from television that some of Chicago's matches were broadcast in Spanish. When she previously played in the States, Dieke was regularly playing in front of 7,000 crowds for Atlanta and would love if Chicago could get to that level in their second season with an expanded league.

"I think in the WUSA, there were three Brazilians involved but this time virtually the whole national team could be playing in the league," Dieke, points out.

"Obviously, they are an exciting talent and the game has come on a lot in Brazil over the last few years. "But there are other leagues in Europe so there is always competition for players from Brazil although there is now competition from America.

"I was the only Scot involved but I know there will be a few more interested. For the likes of Kim Little, I can see her playing in America within the next few years.

"Nothing can beat training every day and getting paid to play full-time. It certainly beats Scotland where you have a job to go to every morning and you're training in the evenings, often in bad weather."

Not that she is averse to returning to Scotland. One thing she was quick to sort out when she signed for the Red Stars was that she would still get time off to play for Scotland.

She points out that Chicago coach Emma Hayes and Scotland coach Anna Signeul are old friends and knew that compromises would be made if there were any potential fixture clashes.

"I never expected there to be any conflict. I've been coming over for Scotland matches for a while and Anna and Emma are good friends and are able to work something out between them," she explains.

"That was another good reason for coming to Chicago. Also, the season starts in the spring, so I enjoy the harsh winter weather as I'm happiest when the sun is shining."

Dieke has come a long way since her days in Cumbernauld but she acknowledges that she owes a debt to her early coaches.

"I would like to give special mention to Carol Wilson who was with Cumbernauld Cosmos for a number of years and has done a great deal for the club and also for me," she stresses, "Without her, I don't know if I would be where I am today."

SCOTLAND HAS PRODUCED SOME OF THE WORLD'S BEST MIDFIELD PLAYERS OVER THE YEARS. THE WORK-RATE IN THE ENGINE ROOM OF THE TEAM HAS NEVER BEEN CALLED INTO QUESTION AND HERE ARE FIVE OF THE CURRENT CROP WHO CAN HOLD THEIR OWN AT ANY LEVEL.

SCOTT BROWN

Born in Dunfermline, the Celtic midfielder Scott Brown is fast becoming a firm favourite with the Tartan Army. Having started his career at Hibernian, as a teenager, Brown developed a reputation as an exciting, adventurous midfielder and was capped for Scotland at under-19 and under-21 level. Walter Smith gave Brown his first taste of full international action in a friendly against USA in November 2005.

He continued to excel at Hibs and made his competitive debut for Scotland in a Euro 2008 qualifier against Georgia in March 2007, a match Scotland won 2-1. A month later, Brown was voted the Scottish Football Writers' Player of the Year and he joined Celtic soon after for a fee of over £4 million, a record amount for a transfer between two Scottish clubs.

In his first season at Celtic, he won a Scottish Premier League winner's medal and became a regular for the national side, producing a magnificent performance in the 3-1 win over Ukraine at Hampden. His aggressive style of play saw him likened to Scotland legend Graeme Souness.

DARREN FLETCHER

Darren Fletcher is arguably Scotland's most high-profile player, having played in central or right midfield for Manchester United since joining the club aged 16. As a youngster, Fletcher had the likes of Paul Scholes and Roy Keane as midfield role models at Old Trafford and has gradually followed their footsteps to become an important member of his club team and a crucial figure for his country.

During his club career he has helped Manchester United to 3 Premiership titles, 1 FA Cup, 1 League Cup, 1 Champions League and 1 World Club Championship.

At the age of 19 he burst on to the international scene with a vital winning goal against Lithuania at Hampden in 2003 in only his second Scotland appearance. Berti Vogts, Scotland manager at the time, could see Fletcher was not only talented but mature and made him captain for a friendly against Estonia in May 2004. This honour saw Fletcher become the youngest Scotland captain for over a century.

In the same month, Fletcher scored his second international goal against Trinidad and Tobago at Easter Road in a 4-1 victory. Further Scotland goals followed for Fletcher in a 3-0 win against Slovenia in 2005 and he was again on target against the Faroe Islands in September 2006,

scoring the first goal of Scotland's memorable Euro 2008 qualifying campaign.

A lot is now expected of Fletcher, given his great success at club level, and the Tartan Army dream that he can be the man to inspire Scotland to a return to the major tournaments.

MIDFIELD MAESTROS

BARRY ROBSON

Energetic midfielder Barry Robson has only recently emerged as a member of the Scotland national team. Boasting a powerful, cultured left foot, Robson plays anywhere in midfield and has even appeared at left back at club level.

After leaving Rangers as a youth player, Robson joined Inverness Caledonian Thistle where he gradually rose to feature heavily in Caley's rise through the Scottish divisions. In 2003, the midfielder signed for Dundee United and, since then, Robson's reputation has grown and grown.

In a struggling United team, Robson stood out as a battling midfield player with great stamina and a habit for scoring stunning goals. His first sample of international football came for the Scotland Future squad in 2005.

In the 2006/07 season, Robson's form hit new heights as he scored 12 goals for United from midfield and he was rewarded with his first full Scotland cap in August 2007 in the 1-0 win over South Africa.

As his free-scoring form continued at Tannadice, he earned a £1 million transfer to Celtic in January 2008. At Parkhead he made an instant impact with some crucial goals, and was considered a driving force in Celtic's dramatic late run to overtake Rangers and win the league.

By now, Robson was a regular in the Scotland squad and, after featuring in friendlies against Czech Republic and Northern Ireland, he made his competitive debut against Macedonia in September 2009.

Robson also played in the 2-1 win in Iceland and the home draw with Norway and would have picked up more caps had it not been for injuries.

PAUL HARTLEY

Paul Hartley is a player who has improved with age and his experience now plays a vital part in the Scotland team. Hartley began his career with Hamilton Academical before moving to English club Millwall where he won his only Scotland under-21 cap in 1997.

He did not return to the international set up for another 8 years. After his transfer to Raith Rovers in 1997 he impressed as a winger and caught the attention of Hibernian for whom he signed in 1999. He helped Hibs achieve promotion in his first season but was soon sold to St Johnstone. Hartley's career recovered at the Saints where he was used as a central, attacking midfielder. In 2003, his improving form earned him a move to Hearts where, under various managers, he blossomed into one of the top goalscoring midfielders in the country. Hartley won his first Scotland cap in April 2005 against Italy and his first international goal came later that year in Slovenia where he scored with a stunning chip.

At Tynecastle, Hartley's direct and dynamic style was a key factor in Hearts' Scottish Cup win in 2006. A year later he joined Celtic where he has added 2 Scottish Premier League medals to his growing cabinet. Finally in 2009 he joined Bristol City

At international level, Hartley has performed excellently as a holding midfielder. His performances in the historic wins over France in the Euro 2008 qualifiers were simply outstanding as he cancelled out some of the world's best and he continues to compete for a place in Scotland's talented midfield.

KRIS COMMONS

One of George Burley's first moves as Scotland manager was to call up Derby County winger Kris Commons. Although he was born in Nottinghamshire, Commons has Scottish grandparents and chose to play for Scotland.

As a teenager, Commons suffered a serious injury at Stoke City and his career did not fully take off until he joined Nottingham Forest in 2004. At Forest, under the management of former Tottenham and Scotland defender Colin Calderwood, Commons grew into a skilful wide midfielder, with an explosive left foot capable of scoring some spectacular goals. However, his 13 goals in the 2006/07 season were not enough to help Forest to promotion from League One, a feat Commons and Forest did achieve the following season. In the summer of 2008 Commons made a controversial move to Forest's local, bitter rivals Derby County.

Despite Derby's poor league form, Commons' silky displays earned him his first Scotland cap in the 0-0 draw with Northern Ireland. The winger was then brought on as a substitute in Scotland's opening World Cup qualifier in Macedonia where he performed well in the Skopje heat despite Scotland losing 1-0. Burley kept faith with Commons and, when Diego Maradona's Argentina came to Hampden in November 2008, the winger played the full 90 minutes and was widely considered to be Scotland's best player on the night. At the start of 2009, Commons' stock continued to rise when he scored a glorious 30-yard goal against Manchester United in the English League Cup semi-final first leg.

SCOTLAND V THE "AULD ENEMY"

Arguably Scotland's best two performances against England came in 1928 when the Wembley Wizards won 5-1 in London and in 1967 when Scotland handed the world champions a 3-2 defeat, also at Wembley. But there have been many memorable matches between the two nations and the fact it is no longer an annual fixture has not dimmed the memories. The clash has always fascinated – an astonishing 149,269 packed Hampden back in 1939 when Tommy Lawton came up with a late winner for England – and the "sold out" signs will always go out for such an encounter.

Here we look at some memorable Scottish victories against England.

Dateline: November 17, 1999, Wembley Stadium, London.
ENGLAND 0 SCOTLAND 1

Craig Brown's Scotland faced "Mission Impossible" as they sought to qualify for Euro 2000. The Scots had finished runners-up behind the Czech Republic in their qualifying group and faced Kevin Keegan's England in a two-leg play-off. Scotland had lost the first leg at Hampden Park four days previously 2-0 with Manchester United midfield player Paul Scholes inflicting the damage by scoring twice before half-time. Scotland needed something special at Wembley... they produced it.

If England expected a comfortable night, they were in for a rude awakening as Scotland matched them in all departments. When Don Hutchison headed the ball home seven minutes from half-time to give Scotland the lead, the miracle looked on.

England looked shell-shocked and Christian Dailly came close to taking the match to extra-time with a header which was brilliantly saved by David Seaman in the dying minutes.
It was Scotland's first Wembley win for 18 years but it was somewhat hollow as England qualified for the Euro finals.

England: Seaman; Campbell, Neville, Southgate, Adams, Beckham, Ince, Scholes (Parlour 89), Redknapp, Owen (Heskey 63), Shearer.
Scotland: Sullivan; Weir, Davidson, Dailly, Hendry, Burley, Ferguson, Collins, McCann (Burchill 74), Hutchison, Dodds.

Dateline: May 15 1976, Hampden Park, Glasgow.
SCOTLAND 2 ENGLAND 1

Scotland, under Willie Ormond, were bang in form when England came visiting, having beaten Wales 3-1 and Northern Ireland 3-0 earlier in the month to set up a Home Championship decider against the English.

Over 85,000 packed Hampden in anticipation of a Scotland win and they were not disappointed. Scotland had been humbled 5-1 at Wembley the previous year and England listed many of the players who had played then, including Gerry Francis, who had pulled the strings in midfield.

There were concerns for Scotland when Mick Channon put England ahead after just 11 minutes but Don Masson equalised seven minutes later.

Scotland's winning goal – four minutes into the second half – is one of Hampden's most memorable as Kenny Dalglish did not look to catch his shot properly but it squirmed beneath the normally reliable Ray Clemence to give Scotland victory.

Scotland: Rough; McGrain, Donachie, Forsyth, Jackson, Gemmill, Masson, Rioch, Gray (Johnstone 79), Dalglish, Jordan.
England: Clemence; Todd, Mills, Thompson, McFarland (Doyle 70), Kennedy, Keegan, Francis, Taylor, Channon, Pearson (Cherry 46).

ENGLAND 0 SCOTLAND 1

SCOTLAND 2 ENGLAND 1

Dateline: April 14, 1962, Hampden Park, Glasgow.

SCOTLAND 2 ENGLAND 0

A year to the day after Scotland's most humbling defeat at the hands of England, Scotland needed a face-saver and 132,431 fans turned out to witness it. Jimmy Greaves and Johnny Haynes had ripped Scotland apart on the Wembley turf 12 months previously, winning 9-3 in a match Frank Haffey, the Scotland goalkeeper, will not care to remember.
Scotland, however, had revenge on their mind at Hampden and that was evident from the kick-off. Within 13 minutes, Rangers' Davie Wilson had put Scotland ahead and it set up a tense encounter in which both teams had their chances in front of goal.

Bill Brown, the Scotland goalkeeper, and Ron Springett, his English counterpart, were both on form but nevertheless Scotland clinched victory two minutes from time when another Rangers player Eric Caldow struck the second goal from the penalty spot to send Hampden wild with delight.

Scotland: Brown; Hamilton, Caldow, Crerand, McNeill, Baxter, Scott, White, St John, Law, Wilson.
England: Springett; Armfield, Wilson, Anderson, Swan, Flowers, Douglas, Greaves, Smith, Haynes, Charlton.

ENGLAND 1 SCOTLAND 2

SCOTLAND 1 ENGLAND 0

Dateline: June 4, 1977, Wembley Stadium, London.

ENGLAND 1 SCOTLAND 2

Ally MacLeod was only in charge of Scotland for 17 matches but gave Scotland a memorable victory at Wembley. The manager's first match was a 0-0 draw with Wales the previous week in Wrexham but Scotland went to Wembley with high hopes of winning the Home Championship after beating Northern Ireland a few days previously 3-0 with Kenny Dalglish (2) and Gordon McQueen both on target.

It was to be the same combination that undid the English. McQueen opened the scoring shortly before the interval with a towering header and Dalglish added a second after 61 minutes, beating Ray Clemence, who he was shortly to join at Anfield. There was a nervy ending to the game for Scotland when Mick Channon pulled a goal back from the penalty spot with three minutes remaining but Scotland held on for a famous victory.

England: Clemence; Neal, Mills, Hughes, Watson, Greenhoff (Cherry 57), Kennedy (Tueart 67), Talbot, Channon, Francis, Pearson.
Scotland: Rough; McGrain, Donachie, Forsyth, McQueen, Masson (Gemmill 83), Rioch, Hartford, Johnston, Dalglish, Jordan (Macari 43).

Dateline: May, 25 1985, Hampden Park, Glasgow.

SCOTLAND 1 ENGLAND 0

There was no mistaking the calibre of the England team that came north to battle Scotland for the Rous Cup.
Household names such as Peter Shilton, Terry Butcher, Ray Wilkins, Glenn Hoddle, Bryan Robson, Trevor Francis and Mark Hateley were all in the starting line-up. The bench wasn't bad either – Gary Lineker and Chris Waddle coming on in the second half.
But this was a Scotland team, under Jock Stein, which had stars of their own with Alex McLeish, Willie Miller, Gordon Strachan and Graeme Souness.
It was a tense affair with chances few and far between but it was Scotland who made the breakthrough midway through the second half when Richard Gough beat Shilton with a header.

It proved to be enough and the victory gave Scotland a confidence boost before heading off to Iceland a few days later for a vital World Cup qualifier where Lokeren's Jim Bett scored the only goal to keep his team on track for Mexico '86.

Scotland: Leighton; Gough, Malpas, Miller, McLeish, Strachan (MacLeod 71), Souness, Aitken, Bett, Speedie, Archibald.
England: Shilton; Anderson, Sansom, Butcher, Fenwick, Wilkins, Hoddle (Lineker 80), Robson, Barnes (Waddle 63), Francis, Hateley.

WINNING YOUR FIRST CAP FOR YOUR COUNTRY IS A PROUD MOMENT AND THE HIGHLIGHT OF A PLAYER'S CAREER. BUT SOMETIMES A SOLITARY CAP IS ALL A PLAYER WINS AND HERE ARE SOME STARS WHO ONLY MADE ONE APPEARANCE FOR THEIR COUNTRY.

Alfie Conn

It is remarkable to think that one of the most feared strikers of his generation only pulled on the dark blue jersey on one occasion.

Conn was one of Hearts' "Terrible Trio" with Willie Bauld and Jimmy Wardhaugh that tore up the record books in the late 1950s as the Tynecastle side enjoyed the most successful spell in their history.

Noted for his powerful shot, Conn was the perfect foil for his strike-partners and, if not scoring as many as Bauld and Wardhaugh, he contributed his fair share – his best being 27 in 38 appearances in season 1955-56.

Conn won his international call-up for the friendly against Austria on May 2, 1956, scoring Scotland's only goal after 12 minutes in a 1-1 draw at Hampden in front of 80,509 fans.

But he had the misfortune of being around at the same time as Celtic's Bobby Collins who was a Scotland regular. Bauld (three times) and Wardhaugh (twice) did not fare much better in terms of playing for their country.

Keith Wright

Keith Wright will always be held in high esteem by Hibernian fans after his goal helped secure the 1991 League Cup in the 2-0 final win over Dunfermline, bringing the club its first trophy in 19 years.

The striker scored goals wherever he played – also notably at Raith Rovers and Dundee – but really made his name at Hibs under Alex Miller. He also had spells at Morton, Stenhousemuir and Cowdenbeath and, at the end of his playing career, spent two-and-a-half years as manager at Cowdenbeath.

He was given his only Scotland cap in a friendly against Northern Ireland at Hampden on February 19, 1992 where he played up front with Ally McCoist in front of 13,651 fans.

There was to be no repeat of the goal he scored at the same stadium just a few months previously for his club in the League Cup final but Scotland did win the match 1-0, McCoist scoring the only goal early in the match.

Wright was replaced late in the game by Hearts' striker John Robertson, a player he had played with and against in primary school football in Edinburgh. Wright has remained in football and now works as a Scottish FA Development Officer with Midlothian Council, bringing on the next generation of talent.

Joe Craig

Joe Craig played for Scotland for less than a quarter of an hour and yet, in that short space of time, managed to score, making him – in terms of goals per appearance – possibly the most prolific scorer in Scotland's history.

Indeed, he scored his goal before he even kicked the ball. The Celtic forward came off the bench, replacing Birmingham's Kenny Burns, after 76 minutes of a friendly against Sweden at Hampden on April 27, 1977 in front of a crowd of 22,659. Within two minutes, he had stooped to head home Scotland's third goal in a 3-1 victory. Scotland's team that night included Danny McGrain, Asa Hartford and Kenny Dalglish with the other goals coming from an own goal from Swedish goalkeeper Ronnie Hellstrom and Dalglish.

Craig, signed from Partick Thistle, played for two seasons at Celtic before joining Blackburn Rovers in 1978 and later Hamilton Academical. He then spent three years as manager of Cowdenbeath.

Alex MacDonald

Alex MacDonald made his name as an industrious midfield player with Rangers and he went on to play a big part in helping Rangers to their only European trophy, the 1972 Cup-Winners' Cup.

He scored a crucial goal against Rennes in the early rounds and was a big part of their 3-2 final win over Moscow Dynamo at Barcelona's Nou Camp.

He played over 500 games for Rangers, winning the league three times, and scored close to 100 goals before joining Hearts, a club he went on to manage and took them to the brink of the Premier League title in 1986 and then later to the quarter-finals of the UEFA Cup.

MacDonald won his only cap in a friendly against Switzerland on April 7, 1976, in front of just 15,531 fans at Hampden Park when Willie Pettigrew, also making his debut, scored the only goal in a 1-0 win.

It was a game in which goalkeeper Alan Rough made his debut and Frank Gray, Tommy Craig, Des Bremner and Bobby McKean also won their first caps. Like MacDonald, Craig, Bremner and McKean did not play for Scotland again.

Alex MacDonald

Doug Rougvie

The uncompromising defender played for Aberdeen under Alex Ferguson during the club's most successful spell. Not only did he help the team win two league titles and three Scottish Cups, but he was also a member of the Aberdeen side which won the European Cup-Winners' Cup in 1983, beating Real Madrid 2-1 in the final in Gothenburg.

After leaving Aberdeen, he had spells with Chelsea where he played in the same team as Pat Nevin and he went on to play briefly for Brighton, Fulham, Shrewsbury and Dunfermline before having a short spell as manager at Montrose.

He won his Scotland call-up in the Home International Championship match against Northern Ireland at Windsor Park on December 13, 1983, in front of 12,000 fans.

It was a formidable-looking Scotland team which included Aberdeen club-mates Jim Leighton, Alex McLeish, Willie Miller, Gordon Strachan and Peter Weir. Another Pittodrie player, Mark McGhee, came on as a second-half substitute, reflecting the strength of the team which had earlier in the year won European silverware.

But Northern Ireland also had a decent team and won the match through goals from Norman Whiteside and Sammy McIlroy.

Doug Rougvie

Robbie Winters

Robbie Winters may not have spent too long in a Scotland shirt but he did play in one of the nation's most famous victories.

No-one gave Craig Brown's side much chance when they travelled to Bremen to play Germany in a friendly on April 28, 1999. But a Don Hutchison goal after 65 minutes stunned the 28,000 crowd and Scotland held on for a 1-0 victory.

It was a strong German side which included Lothar Matthaus, Jens Nowotny and Oliver Bierhoff but, less than two months later, Scotland went to the Faroe Islands and could only draw 1-1 in a European Championship qualifier.

Against Germany, Winters came on as a second-half substitute, shortly after Hutchison's goal, as Scotland also gave debuts to Hearts' duo Paul Ritchie and Colin Cameron.

Winters made his name at Dundee United and then Aberdeen and had a successful spell with SK Brann in Norway, helping them to the Norwegian Cup and also the league title and scored a respectable 70 goals in 178 matches.

SCOTLAND FACTS

Henry Renny-Tailyour and Arthur Kinnaird become the first Anglo-Scots to play for Scotland – back in 1873. Renny-Tailyour played for the Royal Engineers, who went on to win the FA Cup two years later, and Kinnaird played for the Battersea-based, The Wonderers. Both won their first caps in the 4-2 defeat by England at the Kennington Oval with the remainder of the Scotland team made up of players from Queen's Park.

Scotland enjoyed a stranglehold over Wales in their early years and won the first 13 matches between the countries before a 0-0 draw ended the run in 1889. It took Wales a while to even score against the Scots as Scotland managed four clean sheets before the Welsh finally scored in the fifth meeting between the teams. Even then, it was only a late consolation in a 5-1 defeat – after Scotland had scored 23 without reply until then.

Scotland's first match at Hampden was a 7-2 win over England in March 1878. Until then, Scotland had played their home matches at West of Scotland's cricket ground in Glasgow. Vale of Leven's John McDougall had the distinction of scoring Scotland's first Hampden goal, the first of a hat-trick.

Scotland appeared in the World Cup finals for the first time in the 1954 competition in Switzerland. But it was not the best of introductions as the Scots lost both of their matches – 1-0 to Austria and 7-0 to Uruguay.

Scotland played matches at Cathkin Park, Easter Road, Ibrox, Celtic Park, Rugby Park, Fir Park and Carolina Port in Dundee in the late 19th century.
A century later, Scotland were also playing matches at Easter Road, Ibrox, Celtic Park and Rugby Park when Hampden was being redeveloped and there was a policy of taking games throughout the country.

The first England v Scotland clash at Wembley Stadium did not occur until 1924 when just 37,250 watched a 1-1 draw. Willie Cowan gave Scotland a 40th-minute lead only for Billy Walker to equalise for England after an hour.

Jock Stein managed Scotland twice. He took charge for just over six months in 1965 for seven matches (won 3, lost 3 and drew 1) and then again from October 1978 to September 1985 for 61 matches (won 26, lost 23 and drew 12).

Scotland's first match on foreign soil was against Norway in Bergen on May 26, 1929 when 4,000 fans saw Scotland romp to a 7-3 victory. There was some cheer for the home support as Norway took a shock lead after four minutes through Kaare Kongsvik. It was short-lived as St Mirren's Robert Rankin equalised for Scotland two minutes later.

Scotland's first defeat on foreign soil came in Vienna at the hands of Austria on May 16, 1931. Scotland were humbled 5-0 and, four days later, lost 3-0 to Italy in Rome.

John Ritchie (Queen's Park) had the distinction of scoring Scotland's first-ever penalty goal. He gave his side an 11th-minute lead against Wales from the spot in a Home International match in Wrexham in 1897. The game finished 2-2.

Denis Law twice scored four goals for Scotland in a match. He scored four against Northern Ireland in a 5-1 win in a Home International match on November 7 1962 and – exactly a year later – matched the feat in a 6-1 friendly win over Norway on the same turf.

Dundee's Billy Steel was the first Scotland player to be sent off in an international – Swiss referee Mr Lutz sending him for an early bath in a 4-0 defeat by Austria in a friendly in Vienna in May, 1951.

William Evans was the first player to put through his own goal against Scotland – coming back in 1877 for Wales in a friendly match which Scotland won 2-0.

Apart from Queen's Park – who made up Scotland's entire team in their first match back in 1872 – Rangers are the only club to have more than six players in a Scotland starting eleven. The club boasted seven of the Scotland team that beat Wales 5-2 in February 1900 at Pittodrie – Matthew Dickie, Nicol Smith, David Crawford, Robert Neil, John Robertson, Robert Hamilton and Alex Smith. Three of the four remaining players were from Queen's Park and Celtic's John Bell completed the line-up.

Scotland first played in the final stages of the European Championships in Sweden in 1992. The Scots lost 1-0 to the Netherlands and 2-0 to Germany but finished with a memorable 3-0 victory over the CIS with Paul McStay, Brian McClair and Gary McAllister (penalty) all scoring.

Ally McCoist scored Scotland's only goal of Euro '96 in England – netting the winner against Switzerland at Villa Park. But, after a 0-0 draw with the Netherlands and a 2-0 defeat by England, it was not enough for Scotland to progress.

Scotland's last match at the final stages of a World Cup was a 3-0 defeat by Morocco at France '98. Remarkably, three of the Scotland team were still playing in the Scottish Premier League in 2008-09 – David Weir and Christian Dailly at Rangers and Jackie McNamara at Falkirk.

INSTANT RECALL (Page 14)

1 Ross McCormack and Steven Fletcher.
2 Four - Gary Caldwell, Scott Brown, Kenny Miller and Steven Fletcher.
3 Allan McGregor.
4 Darren Fletcher.
5 Kirk Broadfoot and James McFadden.
6 Skopje, Macedonia.
7 0-0.
8 Michael Stewart (Hearts).
9 Darren Barr (Falkirk) and Kris Commons (Derby County).
10 Croatia.
11 Kenny Miller - in the 1-1 draw with Croatia.
12 Allan McGregor and Craig Gordon share the distinction having played a half each in the 0-0 draw with Northern Ireland.
13 False - it was in Amsterdam.
14 It was against the United States in a challenge match at Hampden in November 2005.
15 Berti Vogts - against Trinidad & Tobago.
16 At the Ullevaal Stadium in Oslo in a 0-0 draw with Norway in August 2003.
17 Iceland - in a 2-1 win in a European Championship qualifier at Hampden in 2003.
18 Just twice - in 1992 in Sweden and 1996 in England.
19 Kenny Miller and Kris Boyd both scored from penalties that day.
20 Czech Republic in a friendly in May 2008 when he came on for the final eight minutes.

THE MANAGERS (Page 15)

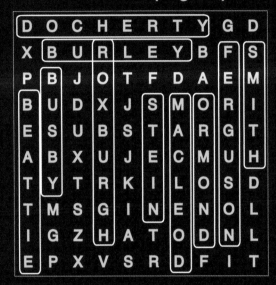

THE CAPTAINS (Page 27)

HISTORY TEST (Page 26)

1 Jim Leighton (91), Alex McLeish (77), Willie Miller (65).
2 George Young (Rangers) between 1946-57.
3 San Marino in 2001 – his 51st cap.
4 19.
5 Colin Stein scored four times in an 8-0 win over Cyprus at Hampden.
6 Four – Ronnie Simpson, Tommy Gemmell, Willie Wallace and Bobby Lennox.
7 Scotland 7 England 2.
8 He was in charge for just 16 months from May 1977 to September 1978.
9 Sir Alex Ferguson was in charge from October 1985 to June 1986.
10 John Greig won 44 caps compared to Billy McNeill's 29.
12 Two – 3-0 against the former CIS in Sweden '92 and 1-0 v Switzerland at Euro '96 in England.
13 Ally McCoist v Switzerland at Euro '96.
14 Aberdeen's Stewart McKimmie.
15 Mixu Paatelainen – 18 goals in 70 appearances for Finland.
16 Kenny Dalglish won a record 102 caps – 47 with Celtic and 55 with Liverpool.
17 11-0 v Ireland in Glasgow in February 1901.
18 0-7 v Uruguay in Basle in 1954.
19 He scored Scotland's 1,000th goal in international matches.
20 Willie Ormond.